ASIA RAINEY-ANI
IYA IFATOLA OYAGBEMI

THE
BOOK
OF
MIRRORS

A JOURNAL WORKBOOK

Published by Nine Pages Media (Imprint: AR Books)
asiarainey@gmail.com

www.ninepagesmedia.com

© Nine Pages Media 2019

Painting on cover by Asia Rainey-Ani (From the *Black Blum* series)

ISBN: 978-0-615-94258-2

Author's Note

I am a firm believer that some of the best things we create come out of necessity, experience, and even failure. Creation of this workbook was born from all three. I have spent much of my adult life giving voice to my stories through poetic means; in hearing those experiences, some people have expressed surprise that I remain sane, am not bitter, maintain motivation, and that I am still here. I have been told that many who may have walked in similar shoes seldom come out unscathed. I do, however, have my scars and skeletons. A long time ago, I just chose to make sure they *meant* something, and I refused to hide them or pretend they did not exist.

With that being said, please know that I do not claim to be a self-help guru. This workbook is by no means meant to be a substitute for mental health professionals, spiritual advisors, or anything else you determine necessary to help you support, understand, and heal yourself. This book is not here to fix you, and neither am I. I am sharing what continues to work for me. It is a work of necessity for my own healing. It is a cumulative process mapped from my journey. It is my recalibration after failing to dig deep enough into my own spirit for answers, then committing to building real tools for introspection and growth. This book is what I have to offer after looking into my own mirror.

In my work as a priest of Ifa and Oya, as well as an artist, business professional, and educator, I often find myself coming back to the same tasks time and again. No matter what I endeavor to offer, I have found that it has been necessary to unpack how I do a thing. As a creative writing educator, I have worked for years to figure out how to guide young students in finding their voice and style.

As a consultant, I have coached entrepreneurs in shaping and constructing business ideas. I did not get most of these skills on a college campus; often, they were nurtured through creative processes of trial, error, and paying attention. So to offer systems for these different types of pedagogy, I developed a way to deconstruct my own processes.

Though often easier said than done, I am honored to receive each skill and therefore enjoy the gift of being able to give those insights to someone else. In the Book of Mirrors, I have deconstructed the process of my ongoing healing. I offer this workbook as an approach to navigating what is in your mirror. However, this book cannot do the work for you, nor will you find the answers to your life written on the last page. This journal is really just the hammer used on the house you are choosing to build - the real work will come from the hand that swings it and the nail you choose to hit.

Whatever spiritual path you have chosen (or not) to take, I offer the same words to you all. May you find strength in knowledge and understanding of self. May there be no wasted moments in your life, because you find what there is to gain in every experience. May you find healing in the truth, which is always the right answer. May you continue to live authentically, creatively, and free.

Asia Rainey
Iya Ifatola Oyagbemi Fayemi Akanbi

Introduction

This is a guided journal designed with the purpose of taking you through an intentional process. Each section is strategically crafted to inform and support all of the other sections in a journey of introspection, intimacy, honesty, and discovery. The Book of Mirrors is an excavation beneath the surface of self.

This expedition will not be easy for some. The journey requires a deep level of commitment to the truth which may be an uncomfortable place to dig, even in the privacy of your own thoughts. In other words, if you deceive yourself in this workbook, you will likely walk away from it with more frustration than progress. If it is a completely comfortable process, chances are you have not dug deeply enough.

So, I want to begin by saying that there is no one here to judge you, no one who will question the validity of your feelings, and there is no one here waiting with expectations of who you are supposed to be. This is your mirror, and you are standing in front of it with no makeup or masks, nothing to prove, no one to please, and no other job except to see yourself clearly. I hope that you commit to this level of inner insight with honesty, and you allow this journey to help you build a greater understanding of who you are.

The workbook will take you through two parts; I ask that you refrain from skipping ahead and trust the process by simply working from page to page. The leading sections, labeled *Guidance,* will first explain your focus for each part; the *Instructions* section will follow with information on how to work through the task. Please be sure to read the *Guidance* sections so that you gain as much clarity as possible around each step.

This process is not a race. Take as much time as you need with each step. Your answers may take extra time to express or they may flow from you in a rush – no matter what happens, let your responses come naturally.

This process is not a test. There are no "right" or "wrong" answers. There is no expected outcome. Every person's walk through this workbook will be their own to discover.

This process is not a spectator sport. I do not advise sharing your responses with others while you are in this process. You may choose to share your outcomes with others when you have completed the workbook, but I suggest you make this a personal journey influenced by no one but you.

This process is not best done as part of a multi-tasking workspace. If time and quiet space is limited, I suggest you think of strategies for working through it before you begin, such as looking for times when you have solitude and peace. There are moments in a day we may take for granted for this purpose. Meditation in the car or on a train, in the bathroom, while taking a walk, or even while eating a meal can provide the mental stillness sometimes necessary for finding the truth in the steps to come. Try to choose minutes where your mind is able to focus and be present in the moment.

Allow this process to be what it needs to be *right now.* From the very first step, you will make choices which will shape the flow of this journey. Open yourself to what your intuition, your gut, or what we often call our "first mind" speaks as soon as you read through the *Guidance* sections.

Lastly, this process does not have a finish line. I hope you go through this journey and discover new parts of your unknown, and then choose to start all over again...go back to dig in other depths. Our work to understand self is a lifelong, ongoing task; with every new discovery, there comes the potential for becoming better equipped to refine the search. The true goal of this workbook is that you develop tools and skills for spiritually, emotionally, and mentally mining your path. Life is a classroom. We are meant to do so much more than just show up.

Part One

The Moments

Guidance

The human memory is a fascinating mystery. We forget what we ate yesterday but remember an experience in fine detail from 15 years ago. Like when cleaning out a closet, I believe we choose to keep what fits or what we think we may need someday…and there is the pile of stuff we hold onto because we have some unexplainable reason for not letting it go. The Moments will take an inventory of some of the items in your mental closet. Whether you grab from the first pile you can access or decide to dig into the bottom right now is up to you.

From our earliest memory into our present, our lives are made up of moments which impact and influence us. These memories range from a small happy exchange between two siblings to recalling the sequence of events in a traumatic experience. Both types of memories have the potential for carrying enormous impact on what we believe in, are motivated by, become afraid of, set as a priority, or even use as a gauge for self image. After timidly approaching my mother with something I'd written one day, she said to me, "Writers don't make money." This experience, which happened within a span of two minutes, occurred over 30 years ago - but those words follow me to this day as motivation for doing the work to make that statement false.

What moments are resonating for you right now? What are the first flashes you receive of exchanges with others, a day someone unexpectedly came into your life, or someone suddenly left? What experiences do you recall which marked a significant change within you or in your environment? For the purpose of this section, zero in on the core of the moment. Imagine the core of this memory as a photograph taken at its most significant point. This is the part of the moment you will work to capture in this section.

The experience may have occurred in minutes or over the span of days. It may have happened two days or 20 years ago. Your goal here is to focus in on and state the facts. To help you write these short narratives, consider these questions:

- Who were the important characters?
- What is the most significant point of this memory?
- What are the relevant details about the experience which underline the reason why this memory remains significant?

In this section, your focus is simply on telling the story. Don't worry about trying to write down how you felt or what it feels like in the present. Make no assumptions about how others felt. Don't worry about trying to concretely define why the moment is significant now; just focus on the facts which made the Moment stay with you. *Just the facts.*

Instructions

From any points in your life you choose, select 5 Moments that hold significance to you. At the top of each page, give the Moment a title (ex. When I lost my younger brother/When my parents divorced/When I moved to Georgia, etc). If you are unsure right away about the title you want to give, move to Step Two and come back to Step One.

Write about the Moment. Talk about who or what was involved, what led up to the most significant point in the memory, and include relevant details which support the Moment's importance to you. When you are done, make sure to go back to Step One and add the title of your Moment if necessary.

Example:

Moment One

Title: *My grandmother's friend thought I was a boy.*

When I was still about a 10 or 11 year old girl, I'd gone to church with my grandmother on a Sunday morning. She didn't drive, so she would often ask a neighborhood friend to drive us home after church and a grocery store trip. I was dressed very casually for church in jeans, a tee shirt, tennis shoes, and a baseball cap. I was also already perhaps 5'9" tall at this point.

When I got into the friend's truck after helping with the groceries, he turned to me and said, "You're a helpful young man. Good job."

"All the greatest lessons live in the stories hardest to tell."
-     AR

Moment One

Title: _____

_____
_____
_____
_____
_____
_____
_____
_____
_____
_____
_____
_____
_____
_____
_____
_____
_____
_____
_____
_____
_____
_____
_____
_____
_____

Moment Two

Title: _____

_____
_____
_____
_____
_____
_____
_____
_____
_____
_____
_____
_____
_____
_____
_____
_____
_____
_____
_____
_____
_____
_____
_____

Moment Three

Title: _____

_____
_____
_____
_____
_____
_____
_____
_____
_____
_____
_____
_____
_____
_____
_____
_____
_____
_____
_____
_____
_____
_____
_____
_____
_____
_____

Moment Four

Title: _____

_____
_____
_____
_____
_____
_____
_____
_____
_____
_____
_____
_____
_____
_____
_____
_____
_____
_____
_____
_____
_____
_____
_____
_____
_____
_____
_____

Moment Five

Title: _____

_____
_____
_____
_____
_____
_____
_____
_____
_____
_____
_____
_____
_____
_____
_____
_____
_____
_____
_____
_____
_____
_____
_____
_____
_____
_____
_____

The Awareness

"I've learned that people will forget what you said, people will forget what you did, but people will never forget how you made them feel." – Maya Angelou

Guidance
Gravity gives weight to all things with mass or energy. In each of the Moments you've chosen to focus upon, gravity exists within the experience and acts as a force. The weight in the Moment is made up of your emotional response (energy), which attracts your subconscious to the significance in the experience. Much like a heavy object falling to the ground, the weight of the response falls onto your subconscious and makes an impact, and remains where it is until either another force moves it or the place where it lands changes.

You are the place where this emotional impact has landed. If the impact is negative, either something has to move the narrative of that impact or you have to alter the way the emotion is being held. That weight can become a balance, a new force to be used to move something else, or it can act as a pressure which holds you in a fixed position. **This section will help you to assess the emotional response of each Moment** and lead into the work of understanding what to do with its weight.

Identifying our emotions can be difficult because this job asks us to face the parts of ourselves we are conditioned to repress or ignore. Some of us, for example, are told as children not to cry, or be affectionate, or talk about feelings openly. We deny an acknowledgement of our feelings for so long that we begin to call them by other names, replacing them with more "acceptable" responses, or even seeing the emotion itself as a sign of weakness...reject it.

I remember countless instances when a boy in my childhood was told to "stop acting like a girl" if he shed tears and outwardly expressed sadness or fear. What happens to his sadness? How many of those young boys hid their hurt behind a mask of anger, bravado, or nonchalance? How many grew up to be men who held that sadness until it became a disconnection, hatred, or even violence? Matter and energy are never destroyed; they are only transformed. The emotions we carry do not merely go away. They become something else, and the question for us is whether or not we will be an active participant in determining how those feelings change.

Instructions

In this section, you will go back to each of the Moments you chose, and you will work to identify your emotions at the time. It is important to name what you felt during the Moment.

Make the connection between the emotion and how you reacted at the time. How you feel about the experience now and what you felt then may be different; right now, the focus is to analyze the impact of the Moment on who you were in that time and space. Use the prompts on each page to help you shape your responses.

Example:

Moment One: *My grandmother's friend thought I was a boy.*

Describe your emotions within this Moment.

The Awareness: *Embarrassed. I felt like I wanted to hide myself, and at the same time like I wanted to prove that I was a girl. I was angry at him for not really seeing me. I wasn't sure if my grandmother heard him or not. If she had, I was angry that she didn't correct him. I was angry that I was dressed the way I was…in hand-me-downs that didn't flatter me or project my femininity.*

Moment One: _____

Describe your emotions within this Moment.

_____
_____
_____
_____
_____
_____
_____
_____
_____
_____
_____

Moment Two: _____

Describe your emotions within this Moment.

_____
_____
_____
_____
_____
_____
_____
_____
_____
_____
_____

Moment Three: _____

Describe your emotions within this Moment.

_____
_____
_____
_____
_____
_____
_____
_____
_____
_____
_____

Moment Four: _____

Describe your emotions within this Moment.

_____
_____
_____
_____
_____
_____
_____
_____
_____
_____
_____

Moment Five: _____

Describe your emotions within this Moment.

_____
_____
_____
_____
_____
_____
_____
_____
_____
_____
_____
_____

Take a moment to process your Awareness of these emotions.
Celebrate your inner honesty in this section.

The Lesson

"Time is only wasted when nothing is learned." - AR

Guidance

Some may disagree with the adage "everything happens for a reason." Especially in moments of tragedy or heartache, the phrase seems to attempt to give purpose to events we feel were senseless. However, the lessons we learn as we walk through these events are vital. **Even the most tragic events carry a message to the characters connected to its impact, visible only when the person is open to what the moment has come to teach.**

In learning the message of a moment, it is also important to acknowledge our decisions and actions inside of the experience. I read a wonderful book by writer and show runner Shonda Rhimes (Grey's Anatomy, How to Get Away With Murder, etc) called Year of Yes. Her reflections in this memoir helped me to name an important piece in considering our accountability. Ms. Rhimes spoke about her decision to "say yes" for a year in her life, and chronicled how doing so affected her path. I thought it was a brilliant exercise in discovering how what we "say yes to" profoundly affects the events in our lives.

This excavation gets challenging here, because one may confuse this work of recognizing our accountability with blaming ourselves for why an event occurred. This is not, for example, about laying fault on you for being in a relationship in which you felt the other person harmed you in some way. **This accountability is about understanding what you said "yes" to in a situation and how it made an impact on the narrative.** Acknowledging how we show up in an experience takes no accountability away from those who did what they did; they are responsible and culpable for their actions. Understanding our choices in those Moments allows us to learn from the doors we opened within the event.

Instructions

Once again, go back to your five Moments, as well as the emotions you identified within each of them. What messages did the Moments reveal to you? What did you learn about yourself, others around you, and/or your environment?

Can you identify places within your Moments where you said yes? What decisions have you made (or not) which gave a person or event access to some aspect of your life? How did your reactions or emotions sometimes shift an experience? What can you learn about yourself in the decisions you made? Use the prompts to help you answer these questions.

Example:

Moment One: *My grandmother's friend thought I was a boy.*

The Lesson: *I said yes to allowing someone's perception of me to influence my view of self. I gave this experience access to the self worth I was already struggling to build, and how I assessed femininity. I believe that this moment instilled a belief in me about my physical appearance: I was not the same as other girls, something was wrong with me, and I had to prove myself to others.*

From this point, I believe that I decided my height and body was more masculine, and that this is how all people would perceive me. My anger at my grandmother's friend was also a part of a shift in my interactions with boys and men; for a long time, I sought approval and attention from them. From my teens into my 20s, I was very focused on finding ways to be seen as pretty, physically attractive, and desirable. I compared myself to other women and desired to be shorter, more petite, more acceptable and inside of a very narrow standard of beauty.

Moment One:_____

The Lesson:

_____
_____
_____
_____
_____
_____
_____
_____
_____
_____
_____

Moment Two:_____

The Lesson:

_____
_____
_____
_____
_____
_____
_____
_____
_____
_____
_____

Moment Three:_____

The Lesson:

_____
_____
_____
_____
_____
_____
_____
_____
_____
_____

Moment Four:_____

The Lesson:

_____
_____
_____
_____
_____
_____
_____
_____
_____

Moment Five:_____

The Lesson:

_____
_____
_____
_____
_____
_____
_____
_____
_____
_____
_____

The Mirror

In the Moment, you identified pivotal events. In the Awareness, you assessed their emotional impact, and in the Lesson you explored what there was to learn from the Moments. **Now, we will use the Mirror to unpack how all of these things have influenced who you are in the present.**

For each of your selected Moments, there was an impact on your character, behaviors, and beliefs. So often, we can miss how a moment shifted our thinking, created a new fear, freed us from an inhibition, gave birth to an addiction or habit, or became the motivation for a paradigm shift. For example, I can remember being in my early twenties and starting a job as a bartender. I wasn't qualified for the position – I had never served a drink in my life. Yet within months, the owners of the nightclub saw something in my intellect, organizational skills, business acumen, and swiftly-gained abilities which prompted them to make me the general manager of the business.

The Moment was more than just doing really well at a job; the experience was the beginning stages of understanding that despite what I may believe I lack, I can accomplish a tremendous amount through the wealth of what I DO possess. This became a belief, a change in my character, and it affected my future behaviors. From that point, I began to limit myself less by what people or even my self assessment gave me permission to do. The emotions and lessons in the Moment formed a habit of crafting my destiny and started a shift in my belief around what "qualified" means.

Now that you know your emotional reactions to these Moments, and you are able to see the Lessons, how did the Moments change who you are? How are the experiences shaping you in ways you have been aware of? If you peel back the surface layers of the experience's effects, are there ways you've changed which have been subconscious shifts? In becoming more aware of these changes, are they all positive and/or productive? How have some served you well, and how have others become obstacles or dogma on your journey?

When we were little, we ate the foods our parents gave to us. Some of us may have been given fresh fruits and vegetables, dinners prepared from scratch with healthy ingredients, and a limited amount of sweet treats. Others may have been fed foods on another side of the spectrum. Both experiences created learned behaviors about how we perceive a meal as fast, delicious, or filling. As adults, we can only change negative behaviors and desires after we first understand where they came from. Once we know the source, we then get to decide if this is who we want to be because we can then see whether the belief was built from the truth or illusion.

We know that a "number one" from a favorite fast food joint makes some of us feel full and satisfied, but feeling good after that meal is a temporary, dishonest high. The calories from the burger and fries give little nutrition, so we haven't satisfied the need to take care of ourselves. Yet we eat it because something in our past built the belief that this will make us happy. So we know the truth, but we feel trapped in the illusion to eat what we crave. Facing the source of the belief gives us the opportunity to change it. We are only imprisoned by negative beliefs when we allow the past to enact them into mental law. Our goal, however, is to govern our mental and emotional selves. Awareness of our beliefs puts the law back into our hands.

In the Mirror, take a good look at who you've become as a result of these Moments. Get to know the person looking back at you now. Understand the house your experiences have built; face how your decisions, priorities, and desires are affected by where you've been. This section lets you see not just who you are, but how you got here and what mental laws are now in place. Which laws need to be repealed? What truth needs to replace a learned and accepted illusion?

Instructions:

For each Moment, use this section to reflect upon how the experience has shaped who you are in the present. How does this Moment influence your current beliefs, priorities, desires, and decisions? What parts of this influence do you feel you need to keep, and which parts do you recognize need revision or deletion? Use the Mirror to discover the truth in each Moment.

Example:

Moment One: *My grandmother's friend thought I was a boy.*

The Mirror: *In the present, I see myself as still struggling with acceptance and celebration of who I am and how I am made. I understand now that I have had to undo this perception and the behaviors it encouraged in me. I think one of the laws this Moment created was to try fitting into social standards. My appearance has become a priority to me in terms of self care, feeling good in my own skin, and celebrating the sum of my attributes as a unique and beautiful individual. The truth in this Moment is that everybody doesn't have to see me for the amazing person I am. The one who is meant to truly SEE ME will embrace all of who I am. Yet most importantly, the one who needs to see me most clearly and accept me...is me.*

Moment One:_____

The Mirror:

_____
_____
_____
_____
_____
_____
_____
_____
_____
_____
_____

Moment Two:

The Mirror:

_____
_____
_____
_____
_____
_____
_____
_____
_____
_____
_____

Moment Three:

The Mirror:

_____

_____

_____

_____

_____

_____

_____

_____

_____

_____

Moment Four:

The Mirror:

_____

_____

_____

_____

_____

_____

_____

_____

_____

_____

Moment Five:

The Mirror:

_____

_____

_____

_____

_____

_____

_____

_____

_____

_____

_____

The Release

Few people actually enjoy cleaning. Perhaps it is because when things are a mess, it is first difficult to know where to start, or how to sort things, or to know how to decide where things should go. In this section, we will do a very intentional cleaning, but please don't dread the work. Imagine the feeling of the space you finally took the time to thoroughly cleanse and organize. I believe there is a sense of peace and renewed energy that comes when you are able to see everything clearly and access what you need. In the Release, we are going to clean out your emotional closet.

In this closet, the Moments you chose are hanging among all of your other experiences. There are lessons buried beneath piles of anger left unsorted, some friendships no longer fit, you've found love that no longer fits or supports who you are, and many heartaches take up so much space that it is difficult to find what you are actually looking for. You have possibilities with price tags still left in bags, untried. There is plenty in this closet which is worth keeping, but in order to easily access it, it's time to make room. **The Release is going to ask you to decide to let go of what you no longer need.**

Your emotional closet has only so much real estate. Everything we hold onto - the emotional matter/weight - takes up space in this closet. We do not have to hold onto the weight of a Moment (how we felt at the time, the dogma or habits developed, etc.) to learn from it and acknowledge its impact. Letting go can sometimes be more intensely difficult when we have been abused or wronged, especially when we hold that memory without some kind of apology, resolution, justice, or closure of some kind.

Unfortunately, for some of those Moments, these things may never seem to come from someone or something outside of ourselves. So how do we let go of a thing that feels unfinished?

I believe that people should be held accountable for their words and actions. However, I feel that we are ultimately responsible for how we feel. The other person can and should be held accountable for their deeds, but no one can make you feel love, hate, jealousy or bitterness, or be insecure, feel confident, or experience joy. Whether you are aware of the decision or not, you decide how you are going to ultimately feel and how you are going to allow a Moment to shape your present and future. Does the emotional space we were in during the Moment still serve us in the present, or can we decide to let those feelings go and hold onto the lessons? How much emotional real estate can we reclaim, making room for something we need?

Instructions:

Bring the titles of each chosen Moment into this section. Name at least 3 things you choose to release from each Moment. (There will be room for more than three, so if you write more, choose the most vital three items when you are done.

Example:

Moment One: <u>*My grandmother's friend thought I was a boy.*</u>

The Release:

I release the anxiety of judging myself by the standards of others.

I release the anger towards those who have not seen me for who I am or given me reason to doubt my own self worth.

I release the sadness of feeling like the oddball, the weird girl, and the ugly duckling.

I release the inner pressure to conform.

I release the self hate which sought approval from people in superficial ways.

I release the disappointment and hurt I've held towards the adults in my childhood who I've wished would have helped me to build a better self image or at least helped me to find the tools to know and celebrate who I am.

Moment One:

The Release:

1.

_____

_____

_____

2.

_____

_____

_____

3.

_____

_____

_____

4.

_____

_____

_____

5.

_____

_____

_____

Moment Two:

The Release:

1.

_____

_____

_____

2.

_____

_____

_____

3.

_____

_____

_____

4.

_____

_____

_____

5.

_____

_____

_____

Moment Three:

The Release:

1.

_____

_____

_____

2.

_____

_____

_____

3.

_____

_____

_____

4.

_____

_____

_____

5.

_____

_____

_____

Moment Four:

The Release:

1.

_____

_____

_____

2.

_____

_____

_____

3.

_____

_____

_____

4.

_____

_____

_____

5.

_____

_____

_____

Moment Five:

The Release:

1.

_____

_____

_____

2.

_____

_____

_____

3.

_____

_____

_____

4.

_____

_____

_____

5.

_____

_____

_____

Part Two

The Joy

If there were a survey asking people what the top five things were that they wanted in life, I believe one of the most common answers would be happiness. Yet strangely, I also feel that most of us don't stop to truly identify what makes us genuinely happy. Even if we do, I think even fewer of us realize that what we choose to prioritize is often in direct contradiction to that pursuit. We may say, for example, that family brings us joy, yet what we choose to prioritize in terms of time, energy, and emotional commitment become the very things that distance us from our loved ones. When we discover or name the people, places, and things which matter most and make them priorities, I believe we should also be clear about some of the things we've given too much space to at the top of our lists. When we can see joy at the top of the to-do list, we then become motivated by what really moves us. Happiness is the biggest carrot on the stick for propelling us forward.

The things that make us happy tend to change throughout different stages of our lives. It is important to periodically check in with who you are to understand where your joy comes from in your present. When I was in my twenties, I loved to go out with friends to a nightclub because dancing made me happy. I loved the loud bass pulsing from the speakers, a good dance floor, watching others get free with their best dance moves, and moving to my favorite songs. Some years ago, however, I walked into a club and realized this joy had drastically changed. I was aware of the "meat market" (being on display for those looking for something other than music) and the music itself was no longer a smooth DJ mix of the hip hop I loved. What perhaps shocked me the most was that I no longer felt the same comfort in a crowded room of people. I could attribute several reasons to this. I was clear that the club hadn't really changed much; it was me who had shifted in my own self-awareness, proclivities, and character. I knew it was time to identify a new joy.

Thanks to technology, I found the shift in streaming music in my own home. It was my space, and my choice of both music and company. The happiness I find in playing my favorite music can lift my spirits, inspire me, or simply keep me motivated through my day. So, I began to intentionally pursue this joy, making it a concrete part of my day, and treating it as a priority. It is a simple act, but it has had a powerful impact on my well being.

In this section, take the time to acknowledge and/or explore what brings you happiness and builds your joy. What are the people, places, things, or actions that motivate you, bring you peace, make you smile, or lift your spirits? What makes your life feel meaningful? Perhaps most importantly, what would give you great happiness but you recognize it may still be missing?

Many of us may first list money. I will challenge this answer and ask you this: What do you want to buy or do with it? Or, what happiness will having the money bring? The adage says money can't buy happiness; I am not debating this thought, but if money is a part of your list, I am asking you to identify why it would bring happiness to you. The answer is not the same for everyone. If this is a possible answer for you, the deeper response is to understand how money will facilitate or be an important factor in the happiness you seek.

Be clear and honest with yourself in this section. Another old saying is be careful what you ask for. We speak things into existence all of the time. Use this section to gain clarity about not only what makes you happy, but why you have decided it is a priority. The answer to the latter will help you to know what your true top priorities should be. It is also okay if you don't know, and perhaps realize in this moment that you only thought you did. This is a great time to start figuring it out.

Instructions:

Identify 5 people, places, things, or actions which bring you happiness and build your joy. For each, you will also describe what each items does or gives to you which creates the feeling of happiness you experience. Lastly, you will describe how what you receive creates this happiness in your life. If you are not able to identify five items…no worries. You will be able to come back to this section later.

Example:

The Joy

What is a part of your Joy?
Writing brings happiness to my life and is a great part of my joy.

What does it do/give?
It gives me a space and time to imagine, create, express myself, share my views, work through dilemmas, document my life, teach, tell stories, and discover parts of myself that are often revealed from within my writing.

What is it about what you receive that creates a feeling of happiness?
It brings me happiness because I can completely be myself while I am writing. I can escape anything that is bothering me when I get lost in ideas and stories. I love how my writing has so often connected me to other people. I get free when I write.

The Joy: *One*

What is a part of your joy?

_____

_____

What does it do/give?

_____

_____

_____

_____

_____

_____

_____

_____

_____

What is it about what you receive that creates a feeling of happiness?

_____

_____

_____

_____

_____

_____

_____

_____

_____

The Joy: *Two*

What is a part of your joy?

_____

_____

What does it do/give?

_____

_____

_____

_____

_____

_____

_____

_____

_____

What is it about what you receive that creates a feeling of
happiness?

_____

_____

_____

_____

_____

_____

_____

_____

_____

The Joy: Three

What is a part of your joy?

_____

_____

What does it do/give?

_____

_____

_____

_____

_____

_____

_____

_____

What is it about what you receive that creates a feeling of happiness?

_____

_____

_____

_____

_____

_____

_____

_____

_____

_____

The Joy: Four

What is a part of your joy?

_____

_____

What does it do/give?

_____

_____

_____

_____

_____

_____

_____

_____

_____

What is it about what you receive that creates a feeling of
happiness?

_____

_____

_____

_____

_____

_____

_____

_____

_____

The Joy: Five

What is a part of your joy?

_____
_____

What does it do/give?

_____
_____
_____
_____
_____
_____
_____
_____
_____

What is it about what you receive that creates a feeling of happiness?

_____
_____
_____
_____
_____
_____
_____
_____
_____

The Manifestation

Guidance

As creative thinkers, we have an enormous superpower to bring things into existence. We imagine and we invent. We brainstorm and we bring ideas to life. We decide something needs to change and we put forth effort to make it happen. Some of it, in the beginning, seems impossible. Yet we have the ability to manifest through thought, will, and action. In this section, we will work to first acknowledge what we want to manifest, gain clarity about why we want it, and explore what needs to be done to bring it into reality.

Manifestation is first visualizing what we want. I believe that a thing only becomes possible after we see it in our thoughts. Then, we go through a process of building belief in the possibility; some call it faith, some decide they deserve it...a passion is generated which propels the last necessary step. We then put action behind our thoughts and fuel this movement with the passion to make it happen. In my experience, nothing is manifested if any one of these aspects is missing.

I once had an idea to open a market for community entrepreneurs, a storefront which housed unique products from artists and craftspeople I knew. I had no money, no building, and only a limited amount of experience in retail. Yet I could see this market. I imagined how the system could work, how to create a cooperative space, and how to align the endeavor with my own interests. I already held a great passion for supporting my community of creative peers. So one day, I asked for a space and started working. The thought blossomed into a project which seemed completely impossible, and yet it was manifested into a space which made a rippling community impact. Without passion, I would have passed on the idea as too hard or not worth my time. Without a clear idea, no one would have taken me seriously or invested their efforts. Without action, it would have remained just a really cool idea. The market manifested from the energy of these powerful aspects in place.

What do you want in your life that isn't there? What do you want to create? What are you ready to change? What motivates you to want to manifest these things? As you identify or uncover these possibilities in this section, you will also work to understand the action needed to bring them into being.

Instructions:

You will list 5 things you want to manifest in your short term future. These items could connect to your work, your personal life, your family, or any area in which you want to bring about change. You will first list the Vision, what it is you see and want to manifest. Be as specific as you can with your vision. (No: I want to make more money. Yes: I want to raise my income by 30% before the end of the year.)

Then, you will list your Passion behind this Vision, detailing why this is important to you. Last, you will list the Action steps necessary to make it all manifest. It is all right to not know what those action steps are...in fact, the first action step may be to find someone who can help you to figure it out!

When listing your Action steps, be practical in terms of what you know you have the tools, resources, knowledge, and/or opportunity to accomplish. This does NOT mean your aspirations need to be small. You are simply naming the doors you already have keys to so that you can begin the work of unlocking the parts of your Vision which will need extra work and help.

Example:

Manifestation One

Vision: I want my household to get to a point of making at least three times the amount we need to live on each month by the end of 2020.

Passion: I want this financial freedom so that my husband and I can spend more time doing the things we love as artists, with each other, and with our children. I also want us to have this kind of extra income so that we can both invest in our artistic/entrepreneurial pursuits, and so that we can begin to enjoy life more.

Action:

1. Prioritize our income possibilities by the following criteria: 1) time it takes to produce the income 2) amount of financial investment needed to produce the income 3) determining each opportunity's alignment with what we are already doing.

2. Decide if anything we are currently doing needs to change or be eliminated.

3. Set aside no less than $100 a month to begin investment in producing our prioritized income opportunities.

4. Set aside a specific percentage of our time each week to work on these opportunities, treating it as we would any job.

5. Figure out who we may need to enlist to help us to propel these opportunities forward, and strategize ways to compensate or barter with these individuals.

Manifestation One

Vision:_____
_____
_____
_____
_____

Passion:
_____
_____
_____
_____
_____

Action:
_____
_____
_____
_____
_____
_____
_____
_____
_____
_____
_____
_____
_____
_____
_____
_____
_____

Manifestation Two

Vision:_____

_____

_____

_____

_____

Passion:

_____

_____

_____

_____

_____

Action:

_____

_____

_____

_____

_____

_____

_____

_____

_____

_____

_____

_____

_____

_____

_____

_____

_____

_____

Manifestation Three

Vision:_____
_____
_____
_____
_____

Passion:
_____
_____
_____
_____
_____

Action:
_____
_____
_____
_____
_____
_____
_____
_____
_____
_____
_____
_____
_____
_____
_____
_____
_____

Manifestation Four

Vision:_____
_____
_____
_____
_____

Passion:

_____
_____
_____
_____
_____

Action:

_____
_____
_____
_____
_____
_____
_____
_____
_____
_____
_____
_____
_____
_____
_____
_____
_____
_____

Manifestation Five

Vision:_____
_____
_____
_____
_____

Passion:
_____
_____
_____
_____
_____

Action:
_____
_____
_____
_____
_____
_____
_____
_____
_____
_____
_____
_____
_____
_____
_____
_____

The Need

Guidance

From the closeness of intimacy to the support system we find in wise guidance, the important people in our lives provide many of the things we need. There are also a myriad of ways in which we must address those needs ourselves. Yet none of these requirements are met without access to us. We decide what we will receive, even when we say something is essential.

Many of us say we need love as a basic prerequisite to happiness. Yet so many of us remain deeply scarred from past relationships, and often enter new possibilities of receiving love with a wall of resistance already in place. Whether it is distrust that has nothing to do with the individual standing before us, or a fear of once again losing someone we grow to love, we sometimes deny the love access to us out of self-preservation. In these instances, it is up to us to decide what the priority is: either to experience that love or to remain safe from the anticipated blow. We have to choose whether we are ready to take the risk on the unknown. We have to decide to say yes.

You have explored what brings you joy as well as what you are ready to manifest in your life.

In this section, we will identify the Needs, understand why these things are requirements in our lives, and make a decision to open the door to what is essential to us. Giving our needs access allows our joy and manifestations to follow. For example, I said that my joy is simply listening to music, yet if I make no time in my day, that small corner of happiness happens infrequently. It is too easy, however, to just say, "I need more time." Exploring the

Need in this section will guide you through the process of naming how to meet the need so that the joy can become a priority. You may have gone through the sections about joy and manifestation and felt you sounded like a broken record. How many times have you said that traveling brings you joy, but you still haven't been anywhere? How many times have you dreamed of starting the new business venture, but are still working the job you can't stand? What was missing? What was the need left unaddressed that would have brought these possibilities into fruition? If fulfilling the need becomes a priority for us, I believe the joy and the manifestation become exponentially more possible.

Some may answer, "I need a good partner/spouse." I have definitely made that statement in the past – and got "what I asked for." Most were good men...just not necessarily good for me! I feel this is an excellent example in how to approach this section. Everything changed in my life when I made one small adjustment to naming and defining this need. The first part was in understanding what the REAL need was. I stopped trying to picture how his personality/appearance/aspirations/morals/etc would meet my needs, and started exploring what I need for myself. I made the list. I then gave myself permission to receive these needs, releasing my fears and dogma, and this partner became clear (he'd been in front of me for a while).

This section is a culmination of your journey throughout this workbook. Allow all of the other sections to inform how you navigate this list. Be present in what you choose to focus upon right now. Once again, be the most honest you can be with your answers. Be open to the process of discovering parts of yourself which may have been hidden until you began to truly dig.

Instructions:

Take the time to name and define each Need. Under this statement, use the How section to list what is necessary to fulfill this need in your life. This list should include ways that you will say yes to this need, give it access, grant it permission, and make space for it. Take as much time as necessary to think these answers through.

Example:

The Need

One: I need intentional time to spend on/with myself. I need time for physical self care, emotional processing, mental rejuvenation and balancing, and spiritual growth.

How:

1. I must learn how to say no when it is clear that I have not made this time a priority.

2. I must schedule this time as I would for anybody and anything else, and stick to it.

3. I must learn to not feel guilty for giving myself the time and space I need.

4. I must stop confusing distractions (television, being entertained by friends' company or conversations) with taking time for myself.

5. I must begin to explore how I want to spend this time, when taking this time works within all of my other responsibilities, and how to do it without neglecting other areas in my life. I must find a balance.

The Need

One:

_____

_____

_____

How:

_____

_____

_____

_____

_____

_____

_____

_____

_____

_____

The Need

Two:

_____

_____

_____

How:

_____

_____

_____

_____

_____

_____

_____

_____

_____

The Need

Three:

_____
_____
_____

How:

_____
_____
_____
_____
_____
_____
_____
_____
_____
_____

The Need

Four.

_____
_____
_____

How:

_____
_____
_____
_____
_____
_____
_____
_____
_____
_____

The Need

Five

_____

_____

_____

How:

_____

_____

_____

_____

_____

_____

_____

_____

_____

The Work

Guidance

In Part One, you started the Work of excavating your foundation. You have taken the time to identify pivotal points on your path, understand your emotional response, and hear the message gained from the experience. You did the important job of deciphering how all of these things impact who you are right now. You made the decision to let go of what you no longer needed to hold on to from these moments. From this work, you wrote down at least 15 items in total that you recognize are necessary to Release.

In Part Two, you also identified 5 things which are a part of your Joy, 5 things you want to Manifest, and 5 things you are giving yourself permission to receive as a Need.

On the next pages, you will list the first 15 on the left and the second 15 on the right. You will find your instructions on the page following your lists.

List One

15 Items to Release

1. _____

2. _____

3. _____

4. _____

5. _____

6. _____

7. _____

8. _____

9. _____

10. _____

11. _____

12. _____

13. _____

14_____

15. _____

List Two

5 Joys – 5 Manifestations – 5 Needs

1. _____

2. _____

3. _____

4. _____

5. _____

6. _____

7. _____

8. _____

9. _____

10. _____

11. _____

12. _____

13. _____

14_____

15. _____

Take time to study these lists side-by-side. See the items you have named which no longer belong in your life next to all of the things you have made the choice to bring into your life. For every one of the things you let go of, you are now physically, mentally, and emotionally making ROOM for what you are ready to receive. Every item in List One has taken time and energy from your being, even if you were unaware of its weight. Every item in List Two deserves space in your life, so as you remove Number 1 from List One, welcome Number 1 from List Two.

Say YES to every item on List Two, no matter how hard the work, or how scary/unfamiliar the newness of it may be, or even how long you've denied yourself this choice. Decide to have Joy, to Manifest what you wish to shift on your path, and to fulfill the Need so vital in opening yourself to it all.

Be gentle with yourself here. List One may hold things hard to release; this Work may be easier written in this workbook than done. If you have difficulty letting things go on this list, be patient with yourself in taking the time to understand what you may need to do to remove these items from your life. Yet know that you have named these things, and once they are no longer hidden, you now have greater power to shift their impact on your life.

The Journey

"…the truth don't care about no pretty lines…"
-   Sunni Patterson

I love that quote. It speaks to the fact that when you are doing
the work of getting honest with yourself and others, you can't
sugarcoat the pieces that need to be seen in their full good, bad,
and ugly. Even while I worked through what was required in this
workbook, composing the examples (which are all part of my real
experiences), and posing every question to myself, it was NOT
easy. I thought in choosing the story about the man who mistook
me for a boy, I was selecting a "simple" memory, but by the time
I did the work to unpack the Moment, it solidified just how
important this workbook was for me to complete. That one
Moment has shaped too much of my belief systems, insecurities,
relationship behaviors, etc. It has sat in my closet as something
I've worn all these years and never looked into this mirror to
understand just how wrong the fit had become. I knew this
workbook was important because it is a continuous, necessary,
progressive tool which doesn't care if you think you've done this
work already. The truth don't care how much I think I've elevated,
expanded, educated, or re-purposed these Moments. The truth
demands that it be seen for what it is.

I truly hope that this journal serves you, whether in part or as a
whole. I realize, as I write these last lines, that as much as I say I
write poetry and stories for others, it always comes back to self. I
did this work for me first. Otherwise, I don't think it would be of
much help to anyone else. Yet, I believe in my heart that
somebody needs this work. Someone needs the tools, the
encouragement, the reminder to give themselves the permission,

the platform to make it all make sense…and the mirror to see themselves in when they are done. I look forward to hearing about your Journey if you choose to share it with me. Your experience and feedback will help this work to evolve and serve others. I can be reached at asiarainey@gmail.com. May your Journey be favored, enlightened, and full of peace and love. No matter what, though, always celebrate that this Journey is indeed your own.

Ase

Giving Thanks

I am so grateful for the love and support of my husband, Karega Ani, and the motivation to leave a legacy to our sons (Karega and Chris) and grandsons (Gavyn and Gabryel). I am filled with joy for the growth and strengthened relationships with my sisters and brothers, all who have inspired my continued commitment to find healing from our pasts. I especially give thanks for my eldest sister Angela, who has been on a new road of healing with me from some of the hardest shared Moments. It's NEVER too late.

Some people call supportive folks in their lives their "rock." I have mountains. I give great thanks to my loves Sha'Condria Sibley, Paris White-Tyrell, Danielle Miles, Tarajee Ali, and a beautiful group of others who are always my examples, my mirrors, my inspirations, my cheerleaders, my sounding boards, my real critics, and my road dawgs.
We ain't done yet, ya'll.

My Ifa community, O.I.D.S.I., has supported and nurtured my spiritual growth from dirt to sky. My godfather, Baba Femi, my godmother Chief Dawolade, my godbrother Ojubona Ifasanmi, and SO, SO many others...thank you for believing in my good Ori, my Ase, and my path.

There are so many folks...from poets to old friends, to amazing community elders and people who have played integral roles even if for a season...thank you for being a part of my human experience while I work on understanding myself as a spiritual being. Love, growth, and peace to every one of you.

Made in the
USA
Columbia, SC